Lend me a Child

Arlene Janoski

Edited by Sherry Johns

ISBN

978-1492808633

Sherry Johns Publishing

P O 586

Penrose, CO 81240

To Birdie who inspired
me in my senior years to
write.   Arlene

"Trust in the Lord with all
thine heart and lean not unto
thine own understanding."

Proverbs 3:5   KJV

Count your days with smiles
not tears,

Count your days in blessings
not years.

Lend Me a Child

"I'll lend you for a time
a child of mine, he said,
For you to love the while he lives,
and mourn for when he's dead."
It may be six or seven years
Or twenty-two or three.
But will you, till I call back
Take care of him for me?
He brings his charms to gladden you,
And should his stay be brief,
You'll have his lovely memories
As solace for your grief.
I cannot promise he will stay
Since all from earth return,
But there are lessons taught down there,
I want this child to learn.
I looked the wide world over
For teachers kind and true,
And from the throng that crowds life's
Lanes I have selected you.
Now will you give him all your love
Nor think the labor vain,
Nor hate me when I come
To call him back again.
I fancy that I heard them say,
"Dear Lord, Thy will be done!"

For all the joy the child will bring,
The risk of grief we'll run.
We'll shelter him with tenderness,
We'll love him while we may,
And for the happiness we've known,
Forever grateful stay.

Edgar A. Guest

Buddy with young friend Kaylinn
Painting by Writer and Artist Marti Fulton

Acknowledgements

Jesus Christ for his love and atoning sacrifice.

Buddy's friends: Shawn, Tino, Mary, Theresa, Katie, Della, Espy, Lupe, and all others too numerous to mention for their love and donations.

Dream Weavers

Ronald McDonald House

Pueblo Chieftain Reporter, Ada Brownell and photographer, Bryan Kelsen.

Sky High Hope Camp and volunteers

Heaton Middle School

Freed Middle School

Centennial High School

Nobel Sysco

Rainbo Baking Co.

Doctors Jarrett, Sloan, and Stork.

Staff and nurses at the hospitals.

New Heights Baptist Church

The Church of Jesus Christ of Latter-day Saints

Charles Anthony Funeral Home

Imperial Cemetery

After the loss of Buddy, I jotted down a few thoughts concerning the grief I felt. Then I joined a writers group led by Peggy McIntosh, an author. We met at the Custer County Library in Westcliffe, Colorado. I was encouraged to write an article which I titled "Buddy's Biggest Battle."

Local writers Arlene Janoski, left, and Joyce Gregor
--Trib photo by Donne Walstrom

Pair of local writers to take part in "Valley Voices" book-signing

The Chaffee County Council of the Arts Writer's Exchange is hosting a book signing party to celebrate the publication of volume two in the ongoing "Valley Voices" series of anthologies which feature stories, essays and poetry by regional writers.

The first anthology, "Valley Voices: Mountain Dreams" was published in the fall of 1997 and included works, as this one does, from authors in central Colorado counties which include Chaffee, Custer, Fremont, Lake, Gunnison, Park and Saguache.

Works by two local authors were selected to be included in the "Valley Voices: Passages" anthology, which emphasizes surviving changes and breaking through barriers.

Arlene Janoski's "Change" and Joyce Gregor's "The Wind Trap" are both poems chosen for inclusion.

Janoski lives with her husband, Raymond, in rural Westcliffe and according to her bio in the anthology, "she loves writing about her heritage and events that have touched her life."

This is Janoski's first published work and she said, "I am very excited to be included."

Gregor lives in rural Westcliffe with her husband, Ben, and also does professional grant writing for nonprofit organizations. Her poems and articles have appeared in "Messenger of St. Anthony," "Lutheran Digest," "Toledo Blade," and "United Methodist Reporter," and she is published in four "Colorado Mile High Anthologies."

The authors will be attending the book signing, which will take place in the upstairs gallery at the courthouse building on East Main in Buena Vista from 2-5 p.m. on Saturday, Oct. 16.

The gathering will give interested members of the public a chance to meet the contributors to this newest publication and have a copy signed.

A second book signing is scheduled for Saturday, Nov. 6, from 1-4 p.m. at the Fresh Idea bookstore on 134 F Street in Salida.

Refreshments will be provided at both events.

--Donna Walstrom

Buddy's death affected me to a great degree because I am his grandmother, and the opportunity to share my grief with others in the writer's group was precious.

Lorinne Gaide, a member of the writing group wrote, "In 1995 I read in the <u>Pubelo Chieftain</u> about a young man fighting the battle with cancer. The story was about Buddy, whose grandparents live in Westcliffe, where I also live. However, I did not know them but the story so touched my heart that I called my daughter in California."

"I related to her the story I had read and asked her to contribute to Buddy's fund in lieu of a birthday present that year. When I joined a book-writing class at the Westcliffe library I was pleased to meet Arlene Janoski, who is writing a book about Buddy."

Eighteen years later I became acquainted with Sherry Johns who inspired me to re-write Buddy's memoir.

"Lend Me a Child" is my effort to tell of the challenges that Buddy and his family endured. Although the years have flown by, the devastation of Buddy's life slipping away still fills me with a sadness, until I remember that God's plan is not mine.

I would not have attempted to write this small book without the Lord's help, and encouragement from friends and family. By this effort I have met many people, and those who I have not met personally, who have blessed my life and taught me many things. For example, I have learned to have deeper compassion for others. I have also learned about endurance from my grandson Buddy, and how to smile and laugh.

Our first grandchild, Walter Steven Doerr, Jr. announced his entrance into this world on March 24th 1978. He weighed eight pounds, four ounces and was nineteen inches long. He was born at Blessing Hospital in Quincy Illinois,which sits on the banks of the mighty Mississippi River across from the state of Missouri. A few miles down the river is Hannibal, the town made famous by Mark Twain.

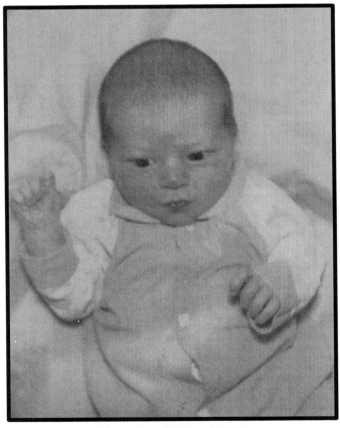

Photo taken 27 March 1978

Soon nicknamed "Buddy" the little boy was a healthy, happy baby.

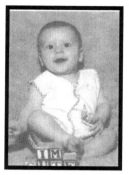  

Three months old   *First Birthday*   *Two yeard old*

In the next few years, a sister and a brother came to play with Buddy.

Clarissa (Cissy) Maelene
Born 25 August 1980
Photo taken October 1980

Shane Vincent
Born 9 September 1981
Photo taken Christmas 1983

Buddy waiting patiently for his new brother to arrive.

Four and a half years old 1982

Buddy's education began at Quincy Headstart School. He then attended Washington Elementary until 1986.

Buddy's parents, our daughter Kim and her husband Walt, with their three children moved from Quincy to the historic town of Pueblo Colorado. Kim's grandmother, Elsie Rapier, left her home to her. Grandma Elsie looked forward to meeting her great-grandchildren. Nancy, another daughter was to be married June 21st 1986. However, Grandma Elsie died on June 12th 1986.

Walt, Buddy, Cissy and Shane

Walt and Kim, Buddy, Cissy, and Shane

Kim arrived in time to attend the funeral but could not stay for the wedding, as her family was waiting to make the move to Colorado. The stress and the long bus trip affected Kim. She had a miscarriage after arriving home in Quincy.

It was a proud day for me when Buddy was baptized a member of the Church of Jesus Christ of latter-Day Saints when he turned eight years old.

Buddy accompanied my husband Ray and I on an excursion across the Rocky Mountains to visit my sister Carol, who lived in Craig, in the northwestern area of Colorado. Buddy was thrilled by the scenery of the high mountains. He laughed at the various names of locations such as Rabbit Ears Pass and Muddy Pass. He also saw numerous wildlife including deer and an elk.

Buddy in the mountains

On one occasion Buddy was watching television with Grandpa Ray when Ray muted the commercial. "But Grandpa," Buddy said, "They have something to tell you!"

Grandpa Ray and Buddy

Buddy, Grandpa Ray and a friend were fishing in the Hermit Lake area in the Sangre de Christo mountains near Westcliffe Colorado. Buddy did not want to leave when it started raining. So the trio sat in the jeep until the rain stopped and they resumed fishing. When Buddy and Grandpa Ray returned to our cabin, Buddy was grinning from ear to ear. "I caught more fish than Grandpa!" he announced. He had caught nine brookies (trout.)

Buddy loved fishing! His father often took him to fish on the Arkansas River that runs through Pueblo.

Christmas was always special for Buddy, Cissy and Shane, especially when their father, Walt, portrayed Santa Claus at Wal-mart, where their mother Kim worked.

Christmas 1991

When Buddy was nine, he had a great adventure. He was invited to visit his grandparents, Lois and Dean Jagger, in Atwater, Michigan. It thrilled him to be old enough to travel alone in a big airplane. He felt he could get out and walk on the puffy clouds that floated beneath the airplane. He arrived several hours later to see his grandparents waiting for him. The Jaggers lived near Lake Elizabeth and often took Buddy on their pontoon boat to fish. He arrived home a month later to extol his family about his great adventure. His brother and sister later experienced the same adventure.

Ray and Arlene   Dean and Lois

Buddy was fascinated by the various items his Uncle Jason sent from overseas. Jason was in the Navy and visited China and Japan often. Buddy's favorite item was a set of Samuri swords.

Buddy with a Samuri Sword.

Buddy was only twelve-years old and he was a happy boy with dark curly hair and a winning smile. He worried about the usual things that boys worry about; school, girls, grades, girls, football, and girls. The girls envied his big brown eyes and long lashes. He decorated his room with his sketches and shelves of model cars. The only thing he had not thought much about was the future.

Walking or jogging to and from Freed Middle School three miles each way helped keep Buddy in good physical condition. Everything was right with the world. However, that spring just before March 24, 1991, his 13th birthday, he noticed a nagging pain in his right foot. He did not give it much thought until a few days later the pain radiated to his ankle and up his leg.

Buddy's 13th Birthday

Was he crying wolf? He was agitated at people who suggested he just wanted to skip school. The doctor examined him. Could it be flatfeet, rotated hip, or arthritis? No, it was none of the above! In June, x-rays showed a suspicious shadow in his pelvic area.

With the appearance of the shadow on the x-ray, the doctor arranged for Buddy to travel to the Children's Hospital in Denver, Colorado where he endured a battery of tests.

July 1, 1991 a biopsy confirmed there was a tumor, the size of a softball on the boy's sacrum. It was an aggressive type of cancer and further tests reveled that there were also spots on his lungs. The tumor was found to be Ewing's Sarcoma.

"Why," we asked "Why Buddy?" No simple answer was forthcoming.

Cancer does not know if you are a girl or a boy. It does not know if your skin is white, black, yellow, or purple. Cancer does not care if you are rich or poor.

Children often ask, "Did I do something bad? Am I being punished?" The answer is no.

Cancer is not contagious. You do not catch it like a cold. At this time, not even the doctors knew exactly what caused this type of cancer.

In 1921, James Ewing, MD, described a bone tumor that, unlike the common bone tumor, osteosarcoma could be treated with radiation. This newly identified tumor became known as Ewing's tumor. At first, this tumor was only seen in bones

Because of its rarity, Ewing's Sarcoma is a relatively unknown form of bone cancer to the general practitioner. In the United States the incidence of Ewing's Sarcoma is 1.7 per 1,000,000.That is about 15 cases per year. It is not clear why Ewing's Sarcoma is more common in the 10-20 age groups, but it seems to be associated with growth spurts. Ewing's Sarcoma is the second most common malignant bone tumor of children, the cause at this time is unknown.

The most common symptom of Ewing's of the bone is pain. Pain occurs in about 85 percent of patients. Because pain is also typical of normal bumps and bruises or bone infections, some cases are not easily recognized.

"Ewing's Sarcoma is a cancer composed of masses of round cells that originates in bone or bone marrow, and may be primitive nerves," stated Dr. L. Stork a board-certified pediatric hematologist/oncologist. Dr. Stork treated about 25 children with Ewing's Sarcoma between 1987 and 1991.

"Ewing's Sarcoma is a malignant tumor of the bone that arises in medullary tissue, occurring more often in cylindrical bones. Only five percent of all childhood bone tumors are Ewing's. About 15 children and adolescents are diagnosed with a tumor of the Ewing's family in the US each year. More tumors occur in males than in females and 64 percent occur in those between ages 10 and 20 years. More than 80 percent of the patients are white."

"There are no special tests that can help with early detection of Ewing's."

Doctor Stork said it is important to be open and honest with your child because if children are not told about their illness they often imagine things that are not true. Children who know the truth are more likely to cooperate with treatment.

The body is made up of different types of cells, and these cells have different jobs to do. Like people, these cells must work together to get the job done. You might describe the cancer cells as "troublemakers" that get in the way of the work of the good cells. Treatment helps to get rid of the troublemakers so that other cells can work well together."

A multidisciplinary team approach is necessary. Surgeons, pediatric oncologists, radiation oncologists, pathologists, psychosocial specialists and rehabilitation specialists must work together to give children and adolescents the best treatment and quality of life possible.

Chemotherapy was recommended as well as radiation. Chemotherapy strikes normal and cancer cells alike, but Ewing's Sarcoma is resistant to chemotherapy and is one of the hardest bone cancers to cure. Treatments can cause nausea, vomiting and hair loss. The Chemo also affects the taste and smell of food.

"Have mercy upon me, O Lord, for I am weak: O Lord, hear me; for my bones are vexed."

Psalms 6:3   KJV

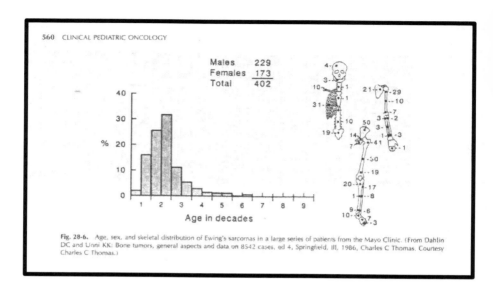

Fig. 28-6. Age, sex, and skeletal distribution of Ewing's sarcomas in a large series of patients from the Mayo Clinic. (From Dahlin DC and Unni KK: Bone tumors, general aspects and data on 8542 cases, ed 4, Springfield, Ill, 1986, Charles C Thomas. Courtesy Charles C Thomas.)

In December 1992, Buddy began therapy with VP 16 and Ifosfamide.

"White milk tastes 'metally' and corn nuts smell real gross," Buddy described with disgust then grinned. *"But you can bring me chocolate candy bars and a Pepsi though."*

"If you were to survive," Dr. Stork told Buddy, *"and your prognosis is only a 20% chance of living, you would become sterile from the radiation, and you would never be able to have children.*

Hearing this prognosis, his family's grief seemed to tear away a piece of their soul.

On July 4th 1991 Buddy sat in a wheelchair on the top of the sixth floor-parking garage of the Children's Hospital. North, east, south, and west displays of fireworks burst in the night sky. From hospitals beds, on crutches, and wheelchairs, IV tubing draped in snaking coils, showers of light reflected children who were laughing and pointing fingers in the dim night light.

The 4th of July was always a big deal for Buddy. *"I want to be home shooting off fireworks with my Dad. Having the usual barbecue and driving around town to see the fireworks. At the fairground and College they have some good ones."*

In the three months following the initial chemotherapy, Buddy's weight dropped from 150 to 106 pounds, a loss of forty-four pounds! On September 6th the boy tried not to cry as he was shuttled down a long hallway to the surgical unit. He heard the term malignant uttered and tried to comfort his mother.

Malignant designates an abnormal growth that tends to metastasize. Metastasize is another big word Buddy learned. Metastasize means a transmission of disease from an original site to one or more sites elsewhere in the body. This is what was happening to Buddy's body.

The surgeon came to explain the procedure to Buddy's family. His white goatee and green scrub clothes earned the doctor the nickname, Dr. Smurf. *"The residue of 21 tumors was surgically removed from the boy's lungs,"* he said. *"We call it Berry-picking! The small tumors were plucked just as a person would when picking blackberries in their garden."*

The procedure was more involved than just 'berry-picking'. It was similar to open-heart surgery, as the ribs were cut, the chest cavity opened to allow an entranceway to the lungs. A mediport, was inserted underneath his skin on the left side of his chest. It was a very painful operation and involved a long recovery time.

Buddy came to know almost as much about his treatments as most of the hospital staff. He was quick to explain to each new staff member or visitor how the various procedures were done and the purpose of each medication

"A mediport is kind of a round thing, metal, with a rubber tip. The mediport is used to receive Chemo. VP16, Ifosfmat, Mesna are Chemo. Ondanceatron helps my nausea. Saline is for dehydration. Septra is as an antibiotic, Magnesium because mine is low, GCSF builds my white blood cells, and because I get mouth sores they give me Peridex."

"Toughest part was losing my hair. (in July 1991) *It really was strange the first time I woke up and found clumps of hair on my pillow."* Buddy reached up and pulled some hair from his head. *"My head gets itchy and sore and cold."*

Occasionally Buddy noticed a fine new hair growth but remained mostly bald. His white count and platelets were on a roller coaster; up and down. Buddy laughed when his grandpa Ray teasingly called him "Bull" after the bald man on the 'Night Court' television show.

The normal scalp contains approximately 1,000,000 hairs. They are constantly growing, with old hairs falling out and replaced by new ones. With chemotherapy, drugs travel throughout the body to kill cancer cells, and some of these drugs damage hair follicles, causing the hair to fall out.

If hair loss occurs, it usually begins within two weeks of starting chemotherapy and gets worse one to two months after the start of therapy. It may come out in clumps that appear on the pillow in the morning or while shampooing or brushing your hair.

"Even in laughter;

the heart is sorrowful."

Proverbs 14:13   KJV

(Cartoon by Arlene)

Humor can be an important way of coping. If the person with cancer finds something funny about a side effect like hair loss, you can certainly join them in a good laugh. This is a great way to relieve stress and to take a break from the more serious nature of the situation.

Dr. Stork related a story that makes the point that humor is an important tool in coping with a serious illness such as cancer:

"A four-year old patient of mine was wearing a wig and was standing in line with her mother at the airport. A woman behind her said, 'Oh, what lovely hair your have!' The four-year old turned around, took off the wig and said, 'You like it? Here!'"

Symptoms

Pain in the bone; swelling; unexplained bone fractures; pain that is not helped by over the counter relievers; unexplained fever, weight loss, and loss of appetite.

People undergoing treatment for cancer commonly experience weight changes. Poor appetite, diarrhea, vomiting, nausea, or dehydration can cause weight loss. Weight loss over time may affect your ability to function, leaving you weak and unable to participate in daily activities.

Another disaster seemed to loom on the horizon for the Doerr family as Buddy's little brother, Shane, discovered a lump on the left side of his skull. Surgery was scheduled and Kim sat up with her son while worry etched her mind. An epidermoid cyst (*http://en.wikipedia.org/wiki/Epidermoid_cyst) was removed. It was benign, not cancer as the family feared.

The next day Kim was going down a hallway and saw Shane, then ten years old, running toward her; his head wrapped like a mummy. A nurse followed closely after Shane, begging him to slow down. Shane passed his mother and laughingly told her, "I want to see my brother." Buddy was receiving chemotherapy at the time.

By November 1992, five tumors had metastasized to Buddy's lungs. He was to face the painful ordeal of surgery again.

Therapy? Yes, there was therapy. Dr. Stork told him that the best therapy was to try to live as normal a life as possible with school and friends. *"However,"* Buddy wanted to know, *"How am I going to have a normal life, when I have to drop out of school?"*

He had missed one third of his school days due to illness and hospitalizations. Judy Beale, a teacher at County High School in Pueblo, was Buddy's tutor. Judy only came on the days Buddy felt well enough to sit in a chair and concentrate on the lesson.

Denver
Heart Beats

Children's Oncology
Services of the Rocky
Mountain Region, Inc.

News from the Ronald McDonald House of Denver   Winter 1993

HOUSE GUESTS

by Carolyn Webb

Walter, Jr (top) with sister Clarrisa and brother Shane Doerr

Doerr

(continued from page 1)

his remote control car, and talking on the phone with his Denver friends. One of his friends, Becky, works on Monday evenings as an assistant "House Mom" and Walter, Jr. looks forward to seeing her. They met one summer at SKY HIGH HOPE CAMP and have been friends ever since.

Walter, Jr. does not mind when he has to stay in The Children's Hospital in Denver because he can feel the caring attitude of the doctors and nurses. He knows most by first name and they all know him as "Buddy". He enjoys teasing and flirting with the nurses, and they tease and flirt right back.

Walter "Buddy" Doerr

Everyone at RMH enjoyed the ceramic lighted Christmas tree made by Kim Doerr and brought to the House by the Doerr Family just before Christmas when 14 year old Walter, Jr. needed to come to Denver from Pueblo for his check up at The Children's Hospital. Kim and Walter Doerr have been staying here at RMH various times since July, 1991 when Walter, Jr. was diagnosed with Ewings Sarcoma. In March of that year, Walter, Jr. started having pains in one of his feet. Over time, the pain became extreme and extended up to his knee and then to the hip. After many different treatments for everything from arthritis to flat feet, an MRI showed a tumor in the pelvic area. Walter, Jr. was sent to The Children's Hospital in Denver for a biopsy which diagnosed the cancer. Chemotherapy started on the 4th of July and he has continued chemo and had various surgeries.

Sister Clarissa, now 12, and brother Shane, now 11, often accompany them on the long trip to Denver. "The trip is so much longer when Bud is feeling bad or throwing-up," Kim reports. But the familiarity and friendly atmosphere at the Ronald McDonald House is something they can count on while in Denver.

Recently, Walter Jr. relapsed with new symptoms of his cancer. "The toughest part of having cancer was loosing my hair...again," he reports with a shy smile. He is good at keeping up his positive attitude most of the time. While at the House, he always enjoys the Nintendo, playing with

(continued on page 7)

"I really miss playing football, basketball, and going to the gym with my friends."

The conflict and uncertainty showed in the Buddy's beautiful eyes as he spoke, eyes that were no longer dark brown. They were now a pale hazel, which was another by-product of the chemotherapy.

The football team at Centennial High School elected Buddy as their team manager. When he lost his hair, the team showed their support by shaving their heads.

School was not easy especially when there were people who did not understand. *"Once in awhile a nerd would tease me. But I have friends who protect me from idiots like that."*

Attending school for half days or even an hour a day – if possible – may make your child happier. Reading, doing homework, or watching a favorite television program or video with your family can help keep the family close.

"He must be a skin-head. He must belong to one of the gangs in town. Just another crazy teenager," some adults were heard commenting.

"A friend loveth at all times..."
Proverbs 17:17 KJV

The telephone was a lifeline to Buddy by talking to his friends about normal everyday things. One of his friends was Tino.

"I was hanging out with a bad crowd," Tino related. *"We thought it would be fun to rough up that kid a little."* This was a fourth grade school activity. Buddy was big for his age. However, he was timid and he did not like to fight with anyone except his sister and brother. This time he had to defend himself. *"I think that I got the worst of it,"* Tino said.

Tino and Buddy became best friends. *"We hung out and did guy things."* Buddy's hobby with his model cars drew them together. Tino also helped when Buddy acquired an old Pinto car. Neither was old enough to drive but they had their dreams.

Buddy and friends

This motto was posted on Buddy's bedroom door.

I know the Lord

won't send me

more than

I can handle

but

sometimes I wish

he didn't have

so much

CONFIDENCE

in me!

Buddy and friend Shawn Gutierrez.
Buddy's artwork is on his bedroom wall.

Buddy's Drawings

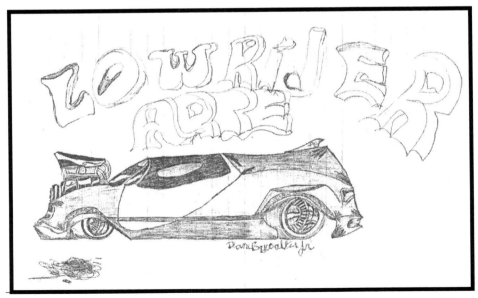

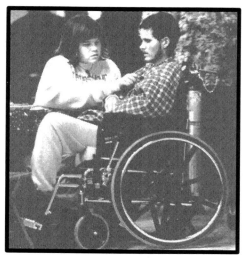

Buddy and Cissy

Sky High Hope is a camp in the mountains of Colorado. The camp accommodates oncology patients and their siblings. Buddy attended every year from 1992 – 1995.

"There we have fun and get away for awhile from our worries," Buddy explained. *"You also realize that you are not the only one with cancer. We went horseback riding, shot bow and arrows. But river rafting was the best."*

Buddy is on the far right, wearing a bandana

Buddy often wore a scarf or bandanna 'Pirate style' on his hairless head because his skin was sensitive. *"At times my head became very cold or it could become sunburned if I did not wear some kind of protection"* He also had a variety of hats he wore for different occasions.

"*The last day at Sky High Hope camp there was a dance,*" Buddy smiled. "*I met a girl!*" Becky volunteered at Sky High Hope Camp because her sister had died from leukemia. Becky and her mother also volunteered at the Ronald McDonald house near the Children's Hospital. Becky became a good friend even though she lived in a different city.

The trip to the Children's Hospital from Pueblo where Buddy and his family lived was one hundred miles and it was agony for him. The pain and nausea caused the family to pull to the side of the road while Buddy vomited. He often laid on a small mattress in the back of the station wagon and watched the clouds, road signs and semi's go by. "*The trip seemed to last forever.*"

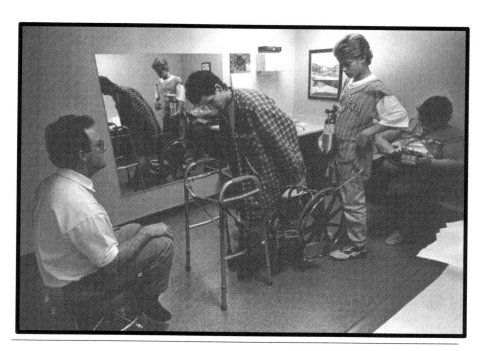

"The Children's Hospital; it's big. It has a lot of stuff for kids to do. There is a playroom with a VCR, TV, and a Writing Board, where I can play with my brother and sister. I can also get a Nintendo or a Sega, or maybe a Stereo in my room. It can be real nice or a bummer depending on how I feel. No matter the time of day or night if I am hungry or I want something special, the nurses see to it that I get it."

Nurses and visitors alike were always tempting Buddy with goodies. He had become tall now but was very, very, thin.

Visitors do not need to talk about cancer. Patients enjoy conversations that do not involve the illness. Do not be afraid to hug or touch, if that was a part of your friendship before the illness. Visitors should not be patronizing. They should not use a "How sick are you today?" tone. Visitors should not say, "I can imagine how you must feel," because they cannot. No one can know exactly how anyone with cancer feels.

Buddy described his nurses: *"Nancy is really nice, a sweet, huggable, lovable person, who will sit and talk to me about my illness. Nina is a short, sweet, nice, funny, kind of person. She likes to play games with me. Heather is a funny, blond, game-playing person, who likes to pick on me, but I throw paper airplanes at her. I tease my nurses and chase them with my remote control car."*

One day Buddy threw a wet, wadded-up paper towel at Heather, who came back with a giant squirt gun.

"An I. V. pole can be a lot of fun. It has five wheels and I like to skateboard with it when I am bored."

In 1992, Doctor Stork advised *"Expect Buddy to have good days and bad days emotionally and physically. He is usually a quiet person and it is normal for him to be quieter than usual to need time alone, and to be angry at times. These feelings are normal, so do not worry."*

Buddy appeared slightly sad during the conversation and bewildered.

"Sometimes being in the hospital isn't so bad, especially when I met the Denver Bronco football players and movie stars like Wolf Larson who portrayed Tarzan in the movie"

An array of volunteers donated time to make the children smile. Clowns, square dancing groups, trained dogs, motorcycle clubs, Jon Court, the race car driver, Carl Kutz who is a jockey, The Rockies baseball players like Eric Young, Jason Bates, and Mike Kingrery, and of course the big guy himself, Santa Claus.

Many firms donate tickets to the Children at the hospital for various activities such as baseball and football games. The Dream Weavers whose motto, "Helping Special Children Realize Their Dreams," made arrangements for Buddy and his family to visit Disney World in Florida.

In April of 1992, Gail Pits wrote the following article in **The Pueblo Chieftain:**

"...Walte Doerr Jr. wants to see the ocean...Blessings happen when the Dream Weavers are involved. Sonia Pinto, 15, Walter Doerr Jr, 14, and Steven Groomer, 4, and their families will be headed for Disney World next month. All qualify for the trip because they have life-threatening diseases.

Buddy enjoyed every moment of the trip, *"I never stayed up so late. We stayed up driving the Gulf Coast until three or four o'clock in the morning. When we finally came home we all seemed to sleep for a week."*

Carmella Jordan, a member of the board of directors of Dream Weavers stated, "Dream Weavers can see their time, effort, and resources, go to a very worthy cause. It is very rewarding for me to see the smile on his face."

The Dream Weavers have many activities; an Easter Egg Hunt, State Fair Day, and a Christmas Party on the second Friday of

December, during the year for their special children. *"Buddy attended every activity and was an inspiration to the other children,"* said Bernadette Santisteven of Dream Weavers. At the Colorado State Fair Day, everyone cheered when Buddy was convinced to sing Karaoke. He sang the country-western song "All my Ex's Live in Texas" at the request of his father.

In a period of remission, Buddy felt better. *"I want to get through this and be well again. To finish school and go to college, be a doctor, a mortician, to take apart a dead person, to examine them, and then I may be able to cure diseases."* He still had hope that a miracle would happen.

Buddy now understood links between his illness and events. He saw his illness as a set of symptoms, and was less likely to believe that something he did caused the illness. He understood that he needed to take the medicines and do what the doctor told him. He cooperated with the treatment.

In June 1995, after a couple of days following IV hydration Buddy was not able to keep anything down and has had recurrent vomiting. He had trouble walking and was weak in his right leg. His platelet count and hemoglobin were both low and required transfusions.

Buddy tells his story in his own way on the next two pages.

It all started Abought ~~about~~ four years ago. i found out
i had cancer in the spine area. it had Been a
Bitch. But half of a year Before that i had some
pain in my lower part of my hicks and then
progressed up my legs After about 7 - 8 months
they finaly figued out i had cancer. All of the
Way long i had to do was the want finely i went
to Down to the Childrens Hospital they ran
a whole Bunch of tests oN me Every thing is probably
scary ~~thing~~ at furst But you get use to it after about
a day. I had some surgery I had a biopsy and
an implantation piece ~~of a mediport~~ of a mediport. A mediport is a special
piece of equipment that goes just underneath the
skin and when you go to get chemotherapy stick a
needle into the mediport But after the sugery
i started getting chemo. Chemo is the medicen that helps
kill the cancer after the chemo I lost all of my
hair. it was in the summer that that happened But
a few moths after all of this thing happend there was
a cancer camp that i was invited to the camp
was a week long hard what i can remember from
that year at camp it was hard i did some horse
back Riding Shot some Bows and arrows and about
three nights Before the last days of camp we had
a dance that was fun Because i met a girl there
That i knew for about three or four years it held
all Beergood after that about 5 orth months
latter i went for a trip to florida that was
fun we went for a week dream weavers paid for
the trip i never staid up so long four the ride

week none of my family could sleep Becaus we were so Exsitied We stayed up driving genuff cazi untell abaut abaut 30r4oclock in the mourning and we usualy got up around 10r8ight Every mourning By the time the week was afier Every Body assured my house shept for week Becaus af the time change wed because af how long we stayed up. About two or three mauthes after that I found out that tere was now more cancer in my pelvec around thay found that out By all of the tests that children hosptle took so Every thing was fine fine about two mauthes that thay found out I had cayre in my lungs so thay started me on a diffient chemo after I staticl a monthor twe better thay did a sugery on me they operd my chest are at children's hospital callied the sugery Barry pickiny thay found a lot of the tumers it my lungs But the way thay did The sugery it was like after burt sugery after the sugery It wes pane full Becaus whin the nurses at the hospite made me walk my chest hurt it felt like my chest dicied a bught al whight on my chest it was prity painfull i was in the hospital for abought week too 10 Days

Buddy, Cissy, Shane and cousins Heather and Aaron, loved to visit their grandparents who live in the mountains of Colorado. Their grandmother, Arlene, author of this book, tells of one visit.

"Hearing shouting and laughter echoing over the mountain I saw Buddy on his black BMX bike cascading down the dirt road behind our cabin. His long legs were pumping furiously on the pedals. Knees bent almost to his chin as he leaned far over the handlebars. Bony elbows at right angles to his body. His face flushed with excitement, eyes flashing. One strap of his bib overhauls hanging and shirttail flapping. A shoestring dangling dangerously close to the bike spokes. A wonderful free spirit, Buddy had forgotten for a small moment his illness and became an ordinary teenager again."

Janoski cabin in the Colorado mountains

On another visit to the mountains for July 4th 1995 picnic, Buddy did not feel up to joining the activities. He could not eat, because his energy was gone; all he wanted to do was sleep. He was totally exhausted and spent

Buddy was admitted to the hospital the next day for red cell transfusion. He was given five units of packed red cells because of significant anemia.

After therapy treatments, he began to feel better and was able to return to Sky High Hope Camp in August with his brother and sister. However, when Buddy's parents picked their children up from camp they realized he was not feeling well and took him directly to Children's Hospital.

One of his deepest wishes was to locate a half-brother he had never met. Walt, his father, had not seen the boy since he was four years old. No one knew where Sean lived.

"This will help Mom and Dad when I am gone if we can find him." Buddy always put his family first in his thoughts.

The family initiated a search. They found that Sean had recently married and was listed in the telephone directory in Salt Lake City, Utah. When the conversation ensued by telephone, Sean was very happy to learn that he had an extended family as his mother had recently died. His mother never told him of the paternal side of his family.

Buddy was on hospice at home with continuous morphine infusion. In October, the doctor discontinued his chemotherapy because of lack of response. Morphine caused Buddy to be more out of touch with reality. By November 10th he was having difficulty walking.

On November 12th 1995, a CT scan of the abdomen showed several new masses and further chemotherapy would not be advisable or beneficial. Since October, Buddy had been on a continuous morphine infusion at home to control his pain, which caused him to be more out of touch with reality.

"It is hard to describe pain. All I can say is that it hurts really bad."

"This young man is one of the most courageous people I know," Dr. Jarrett commented

Two weeks before Thanksgiving, in November 1995, the family gathered to say their farewells. Sean and his wife Annie travelled from Utah to attend. Although in great pain, Buddy refused to sit in the wheelchair, but managed to stand for the family photos. He refused to use the potty chair. Even with his father's help, it was difficult for Buddy to move with the extreme pain and long oxygen tube snaking around his feet. Death was in the atmosphere despite the family trying to remain cheerful.

Four years and four months after the original diagnosis of Ewing's Sarcoma, on November 14th, Buddy was admitted to Parkview Episcopal Hospital in Pueblo. The family met with Doctor Jarrett.

"At most he has two months to live. The cancer has spread throughout Buddy's body. The only thing that can be done now is to keep him pain free and comfortable as possible." In other words, the doctor was telling us to take Buddy home and prepare for him to die.

It was time now to start letting Buddy go.

"What time I am afraid,
I will trust in thee."
Proverbs 56:3 KJV

On November 29, the family gathered and talked quietly about Buddy's situation, not realizing that he was awake and could hear the conversation. He opened his eyes and shocked us by asking, *"Who is going to embalm me?"*

Buddy became involved in every detail of his impending death. Having definite ideas about his funeral, he arranged how he wanted everything done. He wanted to spare his parents, especially his mother, so he planned his own funeral down to the last detail.

Buddy also had help from another special friend, Shawn Guiterrez, who suffered from leukemia. They had met at the hospital when undergoing treatment. Shawn donated $500 to start a fund for Buddy to buy a casket when he found that his father was disabled. *"I don't want my friend buried in a cardboard box."*

Shawn was willing to share $500 with Buddy from a donation fund of $5,000, to help the Gutierrez family, during Shawn's illness. Shawn Gutierrez received a Martin Luther King Jr. Humanitarian award for his generous heart. On January 9th 1996, after Buddy died, the **Pueblo Chieftain** published an article. Many people poured out their hearts with love and donations. Buddy's death affected numerous people

In early December, the Pueblo Bikers Toy Run was held in Memorial Hall. One thousand bikers attended, with packages tied onto their motorcycles. Volunteers set up tables as wrapping stations and asked each gift-bearer, *"For a boy or girl?"* as they wielded paper, scissors and tape.

According to the **Pueblo Chieftain**, Mrs. Sanchez, a volunteer wrapper, said *"I've already warned my family this year not to expect presents. I'm giving my Christmas money to those two boys."* She was referring to Shawn Guiterrez and Walter Doerr Jr.

Just a day later the **Pueblo Chieftain** ran a story about the students at Heaton Middle School who raised almost $5000, to help the two families. One of the students remarked, *"People can't say no to something like this."*

'Bud' Doerr fund-raising dinner slated on Dec. 18

By ADA BROWNELL

The Pueblo Chieftain

A fund-raising dinner for Walter "Bud" Doerr will be held from 5 to 8 p.m. Dec. 18 at Centennial High School.

It is being organized by Claudette Venturi and Dorene Rinn, who work in the office of Michael Jarrett, Walter's doctor.

"We've watched Bud during the years," Ms. Venturi said. "He's an outstanding young man. We know the family and how needy they are, so Doreen and I decided to do it."

The women expected to do a small church dinner at first, but then things began to grow. Nobel-Sysco has donated all the meatballs, sauce and spaghetti. Rainbo Baking Co. donated all the bread, and Coca-Cola all the drinks.

New Heights Baptist Church members are donating time and help, and Centennial High School students are distributing fliers and helping serve and clean up.

Cost of the dinner is $4.99 for adults and $2.50 for children.

About $1,700 has been raised so far to help the Doerr family, principally to help with Walter's funeral expenses.

Walter, 17, a cancer victim, is planning his own service because doctors have told him there is nothing more they can do.

The fund was started with $500 donated by Shaun Gutierrez, 15, a leukemia victim. Puebloans donated money to help Shaun, and Heaton Middle School students raised more than $5,000 to help the Gutierrez family with expenses.

The two boys met at a Denver hospital while undergoing treatments.

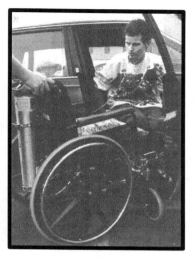

Buddy - December 1995

Buddy's sense of humor sustained him to the very end. He chose his brother, sister, and close 'girl' friends to be his pallbearers. Then he chose sweatshirts for them to wear that displayed either Bugs Bunny or the Tasmanian devil on the front of the shirt and a dove flying away with his name under it on the back of the shirts. The pallbearers wore these shirts at his funeral.

The songs "Wind beneath My Wings", "One Sweet Day", and "It's So Hard to Say Goodbye to Yesterday" were the songs Buddy chose for a friend from church to sing at his funeral. He also asked his grandfather Dean Jagger and his grandmother Arlene Janoski to give the eulogy, then Buddy chose a favorite drawing of his, which was later etched on the back of his tombstone.

On Christmas Eve 1995, Kim called the doctor, stating that Buddy was having more pain on the right side of his chest. Buddy was taken to the emergency room where a chest x-ray revealed the presence of a pleural effusion and was admitted to Parkview Episcopal Hospital.

Buddy's sunken eyes looked bruised and his skin was chalky. Fluid on his lungs was drowning him which increased his breathing difficulty. On December 27th, three months before his eighteenth birthday, Buddy's mother held his hand for the last time.

"I am sorry," Buddy murmured and closed his eyes.

God lent us this child for a time. Now his purpose on earth was completed. Buddy fought long and hard against his foe, Ewing's Sarcoma. His struggle was over; there was no more pain. Buddy was going to his heavenly home, leaving his family with their grief and memories.

Buddy and Kim December 27th 1995

From the **Pueblo Chieftain** December 28th 1995, by Ada Brownell:

"The pain has stopped for Walter "Bud" Doerr Jr. Bud died Wednesday afternoon at Parkview Episcopal Hospital. Bud had Ewings's Sarcoma, a cancer with tumors in his pelvic area, that after a brief remission, spread to his lungs.

"Bud celebrated Christmas with his family when out-of-town relatives were here earlier in December. 'This young man is one of the most courageous people I know,' said Dr. Michael Jarrett, the Doerr family physician. 'He handled adversity with humor. He had realistic acceptance. He was the strongest of all of us...'"

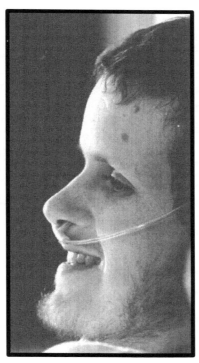

"Father, thy will be done."

"Funerals should be for old people who have lived their lives," Grandpa Joe, Ray's father, blurted out when we entered his room a few days before Buddy's funeral.

"What do you mean, Grandpa?" I asked my father-in-law.

"I had a strange dream," he answered. *"A dream that a young person in our family is dying. I should know who it is, but I just don't know."*

The family agreed that no one would tell Grandpa the truth. We hoped we were doing the right thing. *"He's not up to it. He's too frail,"* we told ourselves. We should have known better.

Ray and his father Grandpa Joe

Anyone who has lived one hundred years is bound to be a tough bird, especially Joe. His stern Polish father sent his son to work at the steel mill when Joe was ten years old. He was just a little boy whose lunch bucket drug on the ground as he trudged to work.

Joe survived his wife of sixty years. Fifty years ago a doctor told him his heart was bad and that he wouldn't live long. Joe survived World War 1 as a Doughboy in seven major campaigns, including the famous battles of Saint-Mihiel and Argonne.

Joe was in the shock troops who started the battles, then withdrew when other troops arrived. A German artillery shell once hit a horse-drawn caisson carrying ammunition to the front lines. The horse was killed and every soldier in the small unit, except Joe. *"I've lived through six wars in my time,"* he once told Ray.

"Why should some young person die when I have lived so long?" Joe believed firmly that dreams were omens of the future.

"Yes," I silently agreed with Joe. *"It's all a mistake. It isn't supposed to be this way. The promise of youth shouldn't have been torn away. The potential of a bright seventeen year old is not supposed to be destroyed. Children don't die before their parents, their grandparents, or their great grandparents. Loss of a child who is so loved is an indescribable agony."*

Joe lived just four months shy of his one hundred and forth birthday, still not knowing the truth about his great-grandson, Buddy.

A blizzard was forecasted for January 1st 1996. Buddy's funeral was the next day. Ray thought we should drive down the mountain and spend the night in Pueblo. The distance was fifty miles, down a winding pass called Hardscrabble, then out onto the prairie towards Pueblo, which is situated at the junction of the Arkansas River and Fountain Creek.

We decided to head out that evening and beat the storm. Jackie, my niece, was following us but took a wrong turn and we lost sight of her. Then we turned back, afraid she went off the side of the mountain pass, but we could not locate her.

Just a few miles down Hardscrabble, the blizzard caught us; we could hardly see the road. Ten miles from Pueblo we hit a patch of black ice. Our 1995 Jeep Wrangler rolled like a Tonka toy. It landed on the driver's side. I was hanging from the passenger side and could not unfasten my seat belt. I guess I was in shock because I started laughing at the ridiculous position I was in. Somehow Ray got loose and climbed over me and opened the door so I could release my seat belt.

A man stopped to help us. He had been up to the dam watching the eagles when he got caught in the blizzard. "It was a miracle I found my pick-up," he told us. Another vehicle stopped and the men righted our Jeep back onto its wheels.

The first man drove us to the hospital. Ray was fine but somehow I hit the top of my head, which caused neck problems for years. Jackie had arrived safely in Pueblo, unaware of our accident.

At Buddy's funeral the next day, Dean Jaeger and I gave the eulogy. I'd lost my glasses in the accident and that gave me a bit of a problem. Even though it was freezing that day, the church was filled to overflowing. The only one who could not come was Buddy's friend Becky.

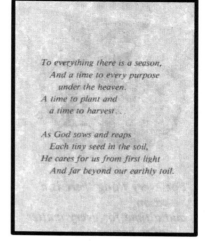

For every thing there is a season,
and a time for every matter under heaven

To everything there is a season,
And a time to every purpose
under the heaven.
A time to plant and
a time to harvest...

As God sows and reaps
Each tiny seed in the soil,
He cares for us from first light
And far beyond our earthly toil.

Front and back covers of Buddy's funeral program

In Loving Memory;
Walter Steven Doerr Jr.
Sunrise   *Sunset*
March 24 1978   December 27 1995
Quincy Ill.   Pueblo Colo.

Services
Jan. 2 1996 2:00 p.m.
L.D.S. Church 1st Ward
Pueblo Colo.
Bishop Karl McAllister
Presiding
Speakers
Dean Jaeger Arlene Janoski
Chuck Shumard Bishop McAllister
Musical Selections
"Wind Beneath My Wings" "One Sweet Day"
"Its So Hard To Say Goodbye To Yesterday"
Interment
Imperial Cemetery, Pueblo

Pallbearers
Clarissa Doerr Shane Doerr Espy Rodriguez
Lupe Martinez Theresa Arguello Mary Toomey
Katie Mason   Della Hernandez

Buddy's funeral program

The front of Buddy's tombstone

The back of Buddy's tombstone. The etching is one of his drawings.

From the eulogy given by Arlene:

"The soul shall be restored to the body and the body to the soul;
yea, and every limb and joint shall be restored to its body
yea, even a hair of the head shall not be lost;
but all things shall be restored to their frame."
Alma 40:23
The Book of Mormon

Artist Marti Fulton, a member of the Westcliffe Library writing class,
painted this portrait of Buddy.

Bud's ultimate struggle

Pueblo Chieftain

January 14th 1996

Story by Ada Brownell

"Walter "Bud" Doerr smiles as he watches his family's antics from a recliner during an early Christmas celebration at the family home in the first week of December. Bud looks through a magazine which deals with his favorite subject, low-riders, during a trip to Hastings. 'Hang in there and fight it out. That's what I've done. It takes a lot of help from family and friends and faith.'"

"Walter "Bud" Doerr turned over and threw back the blankets. Another clump of dark hair lay on the pillow beside his head, but this time that wasn't a concern. The teen-ager was thinking about the sickness in his stomach from the chemotherapy treatments. A hungry feeling gnawed, nevertheless. But how could he eat with the sores in his mouth? Liquid nutritional supplements were getting more and more disgusting. As he got up, the familiar pain shot down his leg.

"Bud noticed a Pueblo newspaper on the table declaring police were searching for the killer of 15-year-old Stephanie Chavez, shot in a drive-by shooting not far from Bud's home. That year, 1994, while Bud desperately struggled to live, five Pueblo teen-agers were murdered by other teens. Lives ended too soon.

"Bud wanted to make sure his life didn't end too soon, even though cancer had been trying to kill him since 1991. He had a learner's driving permit in his billfold, and he intended to use it, and

do much more. The youth wanted doctors to go after the cancerous cells siphoning his healthy flesh and building life-sucking tumors elsewhere. His passion for life didn't diminish, even when he couldn't tell whether treatments were friend or foe.

" 'Just because you're going through something that's hard, that doesn't mean you have to give up,' he said.

"Bud grew up big for his age, but was never a fighter until he began struggling with a disease. When kids picked on him, his parents, Kim and Walter Doerr Sr., had to tell him to fight back. 'You have to let it be known you won't take any garbage,' said Mrs. Doerr.

"A quiet kid, Bud had trouble making friends when the family moved here when he was 8 years old. Fortino Romero, now 19 and a Parkview Hospital employee, remembers the first time he saw Bud. 'I was in fourth grade and hanging around with a bad kid in the neighborhood. We saw Bud and had the bright idea to rough him up. I think I got the worst end of the deal. Afterward, his mom talked to my mom, and we became good friends.'

"The boys used to hang out and torment Bud's younger brother and sister. They went to the mall. They rode bikes. They spent the night at each other's houses, and talked about girls. 'Guy things,' Fortino said. Later, Fortino helped Bud sand the old Pinto he was fixing up, but he never shared Bud's love for cars.

"Bud was 13 when the pain began. Six months later, July 3, 1991, doctors found the cause. 'Bud has a tumor the size of a softball in his pelvis,' Dr. Jarvis said.

"The house was filled with weeping when Mrs. Doerr told her husband and Clarissa and Shane. 'Is Bud going to die?' Clarissa asked.

"The next Friday, five physicians at Children's Hospital in Denver gave the diagnosis: Ewings Sarcoma, a rare lethal cancer that affects about 200 people a year, usually males between the ages of 10 and 25. Doctors wanted to remove Bud's leg and pan of the pelvis. 'No,' Bud said.

"The youngster was in a bean bag watching cartoons when a doctor asked if Bud had a chest X-ray. The X-ray showed 21 tumors in Bud's lungs, so there was no point in taking off the leg. A lung transplant wasn't feasible either.

"All I heard was crying when she called to tell me," recalled Doerr, a disabled roofer who stayed home with the younger children.

Doerr didn't sleep at all the first night. 'You find a corner, you sink to the floor and cry,' Mrs. Doerr said. 'You ask God why. You cry yourself to sleep. People get the idea kids aren't supposed to get cancer, but it does happen.'

"Fortino was frightened when he learned of Bud's illness. 'But then I figured he needed me to be there for him. Bud never cried or struck out.' Fortino could see the anger and fear in Bud's eyes.

"Dream Weavers sent Bud and his family for six days to Disney World in April 1992. 'Oh, we had fun,' said Doerr, a twinkle in the dark eyes Bud inherited. After Disney World closed, they drove around the huge theme park in their golf cart until the wee hours of the morning. 'We saw an alligator and a big lizard crawling across the street,' said Mrs. Doerr. 'That was an armadillo,' Bud corrected.

"Mrs. Doerr remembers the rental minivan. 'I think it cost about $26,000,' she said. 'That's three times what I paid for my house.'

"I'd love to get a van for Bud," said Doerr. "I've got one with a blown engine in it."

"The family still marvels at the elaborate hotel rooms. In comparison, their small three-bedroom clapboard house in Hyde Park, a low-income, mostly Hispanic neighborhood, is inviting because of the people who live there, not because of its architecture and furnishings. The home often is crammed with family and friends, a source of comfort and strength. An 800 number kept doctors and nurses at Children's Hospital, a phone call away, too.

"Chemotherapy and radiation the first year put the cancer in remission for three months, then it returned in the lungs. Another year of treatments, and no cancer was detected for six months. It recurred in May 1994 and he was back to radiation and chemotherapy again.

"Bud's thick dark hair came and went with the treatments, a few experimental. 'Some of the drugs hadn't even been approved yet,' said Doerr. Mrs. Doerr always managed to laugh, even when there were tears, and Bud's own sense of humor helped enliven many a hospital wing.

"It was in Children's Hospital in Denver last June when Bud was doing quite well when he met Shaun Gutierrez, 15, a Pueblo youth *suffering from two types of leukemia. 'Bud was healthy then, and I wasn't doing so good,' said Shaun. 'He was there for me.'*

"At home, Bud customized model cars and covered his bedroom walls with his pencil drawings of low riders. He hoped to finish high school. During his freshman year, he was well enough to go to school all year. The next year, he went a half year, off and on, and the football coach made him a team manager since Bud couldn't play.

"He was unable to enroll in high school last September. 'I wanted to get my GED,' he said. 'But it's hard tutoring.' If suddenly he were well, Bud said school would be the first thing on his agenda. If he could live, Bud would have liked to be a pediatric oncologist so he could work with children with cancer.

"Most nights, he sat up late in the living room recliner, watching folks on television who never really die. Many hours were spent in space with "Star Trek: The Next Generation" characters Warf, Jean Luc Picard and Data.

"In November, Oncologist Marlow Sloan told them there was nothing more medical science could do. Oxygen and a morphine pump were prescribed, monitored day and night by Dad Doerr. 'Just make him comfortable,' Sloan said.

"The last chemotherapy made Bud so ill he stayed in his room for days, wrestling with nausea. Determination and encouragement brought him out while he was still learning to cope with the walker, the wheelchair, a leg brace, tubes, and the diagnosis. His body became like an old man's, but the inner youthful spirit remained.

"The family had been in contact with the Sangre de Cristo Hospice off and on, and Bud learned early to delight himself in life, even though destined for death. 'We help them come to the realization that something is going on, without giving up hope,' explained Sister Mary Conter, hospice director of spiritual care.

Bud savored his life to the last taste. 'I want to live as long as I can,' he said. 'It's probably harder knowing you're going to go, but this way is better than going in a car accident or being shot, because you can prepare for it. Hang in there and fight it out. That's what I've done. It takes a lot of help from family and friends and faith. Yeah. Faith helps you face what's ahead.'

"As the illness intensified, Bud's words became fewer. He would add a few words here and there to an ongoing conversation, but he usually didn't initiate it. The pain sometimes made him irritable, especially if someone bumped the leg where the tumor pushed against the sciatic nerve. 'Without the morphine, this kind of pain would not be tolerable,' he said.

"The family celebrated Christmas early with visiting relatives, and on Christmas Eve, Bud was admitted to Parkview Episcopal Hospital because of fluid in the lungs. Two days later, as his mother stood by his bedside, the tumors and the fluid took up the last breathing space.

"Not yet, Bud!" his mother pleaded.

"I'm sorry," said Bud, unable to get any more air.

"Don't be sorry," Mom said.

"A few seconds later, he was gone.

"Dad and brother and sister arrived a minute or so afterward.

'No! No!' Clarissa screamed. 'I love you!' Comforters came. Hugs were everywhere. Tears flowed from swollen eyes, but by Jan. 2, when the white hearse pulled up to the church, the family was near acceptance.

"An icy wind chilled friends and family as the city defrosted from an overnight snowstorm. Bud lay in the steel blue casket embroidered and engraved with doves in flight and the words 'Going Home.'

"Bud's friend, Shaun Gutierrez, made sure Bud had the coffin he wanted. 'I didn't want him being buried in a cardboard box,' said Shaun, who gave $500 to start a fund for Bud out of money donated to the Gutierrez family to help with leukemia-related expenses. Big-hearted Puebloans gave enough for the funeral Bud planned, burial, and a headstone engraved with one of Bud's drawings.

"Bud, like his pall bearers (Bud's brother, Shane and eight teen girls, including his sister, Clarissa), wore a Looney Tunes T-shirt with a colorful image of Taz, the Tazmanian Devil, the whirling cartoon character that devours everything in sight. Bugs Bunny smiled from some shirts.

"'Bud wanted all these women to carry him to his final resting place,' said Dad Doerr, smiling.

"As shivering mourners left the cemetery, a car stereo blared, 'I know you're looking down on me from Heaven.' The earth soon swallowed the coffin.

"Bud's words a few days earlier seemed to echo among the pines and the quiet of the approaching night, 'I don't want people to be sad.'

"'He told us to 'think of happy things' " said Clarissa, who says Bud is her hero and she hopes to follow in his footsteps and be an artist. Bud bought Shane an erector-like building set, and Shane hopes to have a career working with his hands. Bud told his brother and sister to stay out of gangs, stay in school, and do something with their lives.

"'I'll be sad he's gone,' said Fortino, who last saw Bud alive right before Christmas when he told him he is engaged. 'He'll be my best friend forever.' "

Generous Boy to Get Bone Marrow Transplant
Pueblo Chieftain

January 3rd 1997

Story by Ada Brownell

"Shaun Gutierrez, the giving lad who started a funeral fund for a dying friend, will be on the receiving end today when he receives a bone-marrow transplant from his mother. Doctors at Children's Hospital in Denver hope the transplant will save Shaun's life. The 16-year-old is suffering from two types of leukemia.

"Marrow for the transplant was extracted from his mother, Patty Gutierrez, on Thursday for the transplant. Meanwhile, Shaun was

taking a day of rest from chemotherapy and radiation treatment.
Mrs. Gutierrez is a five out of six match for the transplant.

"According to Shaun's aunt, Diana Gurule, doctors have been
listing Shaun's condition as 'fragile,' but he did as well as could be
expected with the intense treatments necessary before the transplant.

" 'He tolerated it,' said Ms. Gurule. 'He was a real trooper.'
Shaun's father, Benard Gutierrez, a King Soopers meat cutter, was
at Shaun's bedside Thursday. Ms. Gurule said doctors estimate it
will be 22 days before they will have indications as to whether the
transplant worked for Shaun.

" 'It will probably be 100 days before he can be released from the
hospital and go back to Ronald McDonald House,' she said. 'We're
just praying real hard for him. He's got such a good attitude. I think
that will pull Shaun through.'

"Shaun, a freshman at East High School, became well known to
Puebloans when he started a fund for Walter "Bud" Doerr with $500
given to help his family with expenses related to leukemia.
Puebloans also gave generously so Bud, 17, could have a proper
funeral. Bud, a cancer victim, died in December 1995."

In January 1998, two years after her brother Buddy died, Clarissa Doerr wrote this story for a school assignment.

A Person Who Helped Me

There are many people who have helped me go through life. One of these people is my older brother Walter Doerr Jr. We called him Buddy or just Bud. How Buddy helped me is he taught me to ride a bike. It was really cool because my younger brother Shane, and a friend who lives up the street, were all riding bikes one day when it was nice and hot. We tried so hard to ride.

One day Buddy came outside and told me to get on my bike. A reminder, we lived on a dead-end street. Buddy said Ready, get set, go! He ran with me then he let me go and told me to "pedal-pedal!". Just then I slammed into the block gates. It was real fun but it hurt.

Buddy was very special to me. I love him and I miss him so much. He taught me a lot of stuff like to love one another and to respect others. He told me to go to school and get an education and to live a full life.

When Buddy got sick I was there. I tried so hard to make him not be sick any more but I could not. The years passed and he got sicker and sicker. I felt like I wanted the cancer instead if him.

He passed away on December 27th, 1995. I wanted to go with him but I knew he was going to a better place in heaven. I promised him I would go all the way through school and try to go to college.

I loved him since he was like a dad to me and my brother Shane too. When my dad was drinking really hard, Buddy was there for the family. When Buddy passed away my mom was by his side holding his hand. She was right there when he was called on by God.

So he is a very special angel, my Buddy angel. Well, the family is ok. My dad is a recovering alcoholic, and my mom is the best. I have so much thanks to give to her. She has been there for me all the way. Shane, I love him so much; I do not want to lose him ever.

It does not matter what people think about people who are very sick or not well off. It is what you believe in. I wish Buddy was here in the present. He is really, but sometimes I prayed to God and asked Him why he took Buddy. Sometimes I talked to Him as if he is there or something. Everybody should understand the consideration of life and death.

Two and a half years after his best friend Buddy died, Shaun dies from his leukemia. The two young men are now dancing in heaver together.

Shaun Gutierrez succumbs to leukemia complications

By LORETTA SWORD
The Pueblo Chieftain

Puebloan Shaun Guiterrez died Sunday of complications from leukemia. He would have turned 18 on Wednesday.

Shaun became an unwilling hero of sorts when he gave money intended to help his family with medical bills to fellow cancer patient Walter "Bud" Doerr, who knew his death was imminent, so Doerr could buy the casket he wanted to be buried in.

The two had become friends while undergoing chemotherapy and other treatments at The Children's Hospital in Denver.

Shaun's mother, Pat, said the gesture was typical of her son's generous spirit.

"I know he touched a lot of people's hearts in this community. Everywhere he went, he left an impression on someone," she said during a tearful interview Sunday evening.

Mrs. Gutierrez gave her bone marrow for a transplant in 1996 that doctors hoped would cure the two types of leukemia he had. Chemotherapy just after his diag-

Shaun Gutierrez

nosis in 1995 brought only a temporary remission.

He did well for months after the transplant, earning a 3.5 grade point average at East High School.

He worked part time as a guest clerk at King Soopers and was once again enjoying a social life.

But in Febuary, he developed graft vs. host disease, in which the donated marrow attacks the recipient's already weakened immune system.

Then, he developed a dangerous respiratory infection, and a staph infection in his sinuses.

Except for a week at home earlier this summer, and for 11 days before he died, Shaun continued battling the infections at Parkview Hospital.

Although he had experienced much pain during the past few years, his mom said, "he never complained. He always worried about the rest of us, how we were holding up. But his poor little body just got so tired.

"He didn't fight at the end. He didn't struggle. He was very comfortable. He had been saying for a couple of days that he wanted to go home, and he was already at home. I knew he was talking about heaven. And that's where he is now."

Shaun's funeral will be sometime Wednesday. Romero Funeral Home is handling the arrangements, which hadn't been finalized Sunday evening.

Buddy's father deteriorated from a robust man to a frail old man as hepatitis destroyed his liver. On April 22nd 2009, Walter Doerr Sr. passed away, leaving a young widow with two children and a mountain of debt. They lost their ancestral home just a few weeks later to a bank foreclosure.

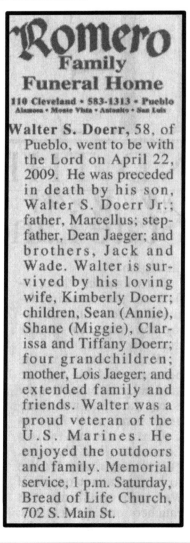

Romero Family Funeral Home
110 Cleveland • 583-1313 • Pueblo
Alamosa • Monte Vista • Antonito • San Luis

Walter S. Doerr, 58, of Pueblo, went to be with the Lord on April 22, 2009. He was preceded in death by his son, Walter S. Doerr Jr.; father, Marcellus; step-father, Dean Jaeger; and brothers, Jack and Wade. Walter is sur-vived by his loving wife, Kimberly Doerr; children, Sean (Annie), Shane (Miggie), Clar-issa and Tiffany Doerr; four grandchildren; mother, Lois Jaeger; and extended family and friends. Walter was a proud veteran of the U.S. Marines. He enjoyed the outdoors and family. Memorial service, 1 p.m. Saturday, Bread of Life Church, 702 S. Main St.

Kim had to make a living and she had to face the rest of her life without her husband and best friend. It was overwhelming at times. *"Why did God let this happen?"* she often asked herself.

The challenge was formidable. Their whole world was turned upside down. They have undergone significant financial hardships and emotional upheaval through the years. Cissy and Shane did not attain their goals as they had promised their brother Buddy. Kim has not remarried.

Sean, Buddy's half-brother, married Annie. They have two children, and keep in touch with the family. Shane has two sons and a daughter and Cissy has a son.

Skylar LeeAnn Rhodes, daughter of Sean and Annie Rhodes

Notes

From the book 'Visions' by Michio Kaku, Henry Semat Professor of Theoretical Physics of the City College of New York, Page 143:

"The intense effort leading to personalized DNA codes is already reverberating throughout scientific laboratories around the world, giving us the promise of altering the course of medicine. By 2020, a map of the 100,000 genes in our human genome could revolutionize the way we treat disease, allowing us to create new classes of therapies and cure debilitating diseases once thought to be hopelessly incurable. Scientists will have a flood of new technologies, such as gene therapy and "smart molecules," to attack these "ancient" diseases. Large classes of cancer should be curable by 2020, many scientists believe."

Buddy is listed as #7881 in the cancer study group at the Children's Hospital in Denver, Colorado

Signs and Symptoms

Pain in the bone; swelling; unexplained bone fractures; pain that is not helped by over-the-counter relievers; unexplained fever, weight loss, and loss of appetite.

(**NOTE**: see your health provider without delay.)

Glossary

Bone: Bone is a connective tissue that makes up the skeletal system, giving the body shape and form.

Cancer: Any of various malignant neoplasm's that manifest invasiveness and a tendency to metastasize to new sites.

Chemotherapy: The treatment of disease with chemicals.

DNA: A code of the genes in the human body.

Ewing's Sarcoma: A malignant tumor of the bone that arises in medullary tissue, occurring more often in cylindrical bones.

Mediport: A device that is implanted under the skin and is used to inject chemotherapy medications into.

Metastasize: Transmission of disease from an original site to one or more sites elsewhere in the body.

Resources

American Cancer Society Response Line 1-800-327-2345

They will refer to local chapters.

National Cancer Institute's Cancer information line

1-800-4-cancer (422-6237)

The Children's Hospital of Denver, Colorado

1-800-458-6500

Ordering Information:

Copies of "Lend Me a Child" are available for $9.95 at **www.amazon.com** and on **KINDLE** for $4.99, or by contacting Arlene Janoski at: **elsiearlenej@gmail.com**.

Bulk copies are available at a discount. Contact Arlene for more information.

About the Author

Arlene Janoski lives near Westcliffe, Colorado in the Wet Mountains with her husband Ray, their cat Rascal, two bobcats, turkey, deer, bear, and many of God's creatures. She cried and laughed while struggling to write the story of her grandson, Buddy.

A portion of the proceeds from the sale of this book will go to Dream Weavers. **www.dreamweaversofsoutherncolorado.org**

Dreamweavers of Southern Colorado

P O Box 212

Pueblo, CO 81002   719.560.4837

Arlene and Buddy on the family land in the mountains in Colorado.

Made in the USA
Charleston, SC
22 August 2015